BEI GRIN MACHT SICH IHR WISSEN BEZAHLT

- Wir veröffentlichen Ihre Hausarbeit, Bachelor- und Masterarbeit

- Ihr eigenes eBook und Buch - weltweit in allen wichtigen Shops

- Verdienen Sie an jedem Verkauf

Jetzt bei www.GRIN.com hochladen und kostenlos publizieren

Bibliographic information published by the German National Library:

The German National Library lists this publication in the National Bibliography; detailed bibliographic data are available on the Internet at http://dnb.dnb.de .

This book is copyright material and must not be copied, reproduced, transferred, distributed, leased, licensed or publicly performed or used in any way except as specifically permitted in writing by the publishers, as allowed under the terms and conditions under which it was purchased or as strictly permitted by applicable copyright law. Any unauthorized distribution or use of this text may be a direct infringement of the author s and publisher s rights and those responsible may be liable in law accordingly.

Imprint:

Copyright © 2019 GRIN Verlag
Print and binding: Books on Demand GmbH, Norderstedt Germany
ISBN: 9783668964396

This book at GRIN:

https://www.grin.com/document/491924

Joefel Horca, Helen Aure, Anna Marie Aranzanzo, Herminia Diloy

Project Teach. An Instructional Support to the Teachers

GRIN Verlag

GRIN - Your knowledge has value

Since its foundation in 1998, GRIN has specialized in publishing academic texts by students, college teachers and other academics as e-book and printed book. The website www.grin.com is an ideal platform for presenting term papers, final papers, scientific essays, dissertations and specialist books.

Visit us on the internet:

http://www.grin.com/

http://www.facebook.com/grincom

http://www.twitter.com/grin_com

Project T.E.A.C.H. *(Technical tEaching Assistance Commonly given by school Heads to teachers)*

AN INSTRUCTIONAL SUPPORT TO THE TEACHERS OF XY: INPUT FOR RPMS-PPST PROFESSIONAL DEVELOPMENT FOR TEACHERS

HELEN C. AURE, Ph.D.
JOEFEL S. HORCA, Ed.D.
ANNA MARIE S. ARANZANZO, Ed.D.
HERMINIA E. DILOY, Ed.D.
Researcher

I. **Introduction**

Having a 21st century learners, teachers needs 21st century teaching skills to address the demands of this type of learners. In this new generation of learners, teachers need to upgrade their teaching competencies so that they can provide the 21st century skills needed by the learners.

In 2012, the Philippine government mandated the Department of Education (DepEd) to implement the K-12 curriculum under the leadership of the Bro. Armin Luistro as the Department Sectary of Education. This new curriculum is aimed to provide the 2 years of backlog of Filipino working class to complete the 12 years of education in the other countries.

This curriculum is also aimed to provide the working class the skills that they need to make them a globally competitive labor force. But, how about teachers who do not undergo 12 years of schooling, are they prepared to provide the 21st century skills to the 21st century learners?

This study adheres to one of the 7 CID projects of the Division of Cavite Province the HI-TEACH which aims to strengthen the Instructional Support of School Heads and Educational Supervisors to teachers to strengthen their teaching skills for the 21st century learners.

II. **Review of Related Literature**

The following related literatures was gathered to provide the background of the study.

In the study conducted by Pa-Alisbo (2017) he concluded that teaching performance of teachers did not vary in terms of educational attainments, length of service and salary grade. He also found out that young professionals have been developed in their pre-service years while the seasoned teachers have been honed through the passing of years though slightly different in computer literacy. He recommends that DepEd should implement the intensive monitoring and evaluation teacher's job performance of from the higher ranks, district supervisors, school heads, peers and pupils or learners other than just mere self-assessment. Sustainability of professional growth among teachers are likewise advised.

Maksimovic and Dimic (2016), found out that in strengthening teacher's teaching performance, it is necessary to teachers to equipped them serves with the importance and utilization of Information Communication technology (ICT) having this competencies, teachers can provide 21st century skills among pupils.

Archambault and Larson (2015) on their study on pioneering the digital Age of instruction: learning from and about K-12 online teachers, they suggested that teachers must be prepared in both face-to-face and online teaching methods and practices.

III. Research Questions

This study aimed to answer the following questions:

1. During the observation process of school heads to teachers, what are the common technical assistance provided by the school heads to teachers?
2. What are the technical assistance provided by the school heads in terms of the following domains:
   a. Content Knowledge and Pedagogy;
   b. Learning Environment and Diversity of Learners;
   c. Curriculum and Planning; and
   d. Assessment and Reporting
3. Based on the findings, what Professional Development Plan maybe proposed?
4. What is the future plan of the XY for the Professional Development of teachers?

IV. Scope and Limitation

The participants of this study are the School Heads and Teachers of XY both Elementary and Secondary with 1 year and above year in the service.

V. Ethical Issues

Prior to the conduct / distribution of the questionnaires, the research ask the permission of the Schools Division Superintendent that she will be allowed to distribute questionnaires to the different schools in the district of Trece Martires City. That research also assured to the participants the outmost confidentiality of their responses.

VI. Methodology

This study employed the mixed method in the statistical treatment of the data and the following statistical tools used to answer the research questions the frequency, ranking of variables, weighted mean of the respondents. This study will also employ purposive sampling of respondents since all of the school heads are participants of the study.

VII. Sampling and Population

The participants of this study are the 28 school heads and 1200 teachers of XY. Purposive sampling was employed in this study. Teachers who belongs to 1 year and below in the service were not included in the study.

VIII. Data Collection

This study utilized Likert Scale, self-made questionnaire and unstructured interview adopting some of the indicators stipulated in the past tools in assessing teachers performance in the CB-PAST and NCBTS TSINA and was validated by one of the Human Resource Professor in Eulogio "Amang" Rodriguez Institute of Science and Technology.

IX. Data Analysis

To provide the specific answers to the research questions of the study the researcher employed percentage, weighted means and ranking of the responses of the participants.

X. Results and Discussion

SOP 1 During the observation process of school heads to teachers, what are the common technical

assistance provided by the school heads to teachers?

a. Content Knowledge and Pedagogy

Use of ICT in planning, designing and delivery of the lesson find ways and means to integrate the lessons to other curriculum areas. Teachers was encourage to be resourceful. Mentored teachers through observation of demonstration teaching aligned with the approaches.

b. Learning Environment and Diversity of Learners;

The school head see to it that immediate attention to queries and improvement of classroom setting as possible. The teachers give enough time to think for the correct answer, the learners was provided materials available in the classroom and not for display only.

c. Curriculum and Planning

The school head conducts staff meeting every month to provide feedback to provide better communications and improvement for the next month.

The teachers was encourage to enroll to have a short courses of computer studies for them to be equipped with the current trends.

d. Assessment and Reporting?

The teachers are instructed to revisit test construction by giving them training on test construction supervise them in the intervention activities that the teachers are doing and monitor them.

The school head Develop SLAC on test construction and how to align the test to Blooms Taxonomy.

SOP 2. What are the technical assistance provided by the school heads in terms of the following domains:

Table 1

RESPONSES OF SCHOOLS HEADS ON THE DIFFERENT DOMAINS

Domain	School Head	WM	Verbal Interpretation	Rank
Content Knowledge and Pedagogy	28	4.60	Very Evident	4
Learning Environment and Diversity of Learners	28	4.61	Very Evident	3
Curriculum and Planning	28	4.62		1.5
Assessment and Reporting	28	4.62	Very Evident	1.5
Total		4.61	Very Evident	

Table 1 shows that school heads rated the following domains, content knowledge and pedagogy of 4.60, Learning Environment and Diversity of Learners 4.61, Curriculum and Planning 4.62, Assessment and Reporting 4.62 with a total average mean of 4.61 which means Very Evident.

Table 2

RESPONSES OF TEACHERS ON THE DIFFERENT DOMAINS

Domain	Teachers	WM	Interpretation	Rank
Content Knowledge and Pedagogy	1200	4.56	Very Evident	4
Learning Environment and Diversity of Learners	1200	4.59	Very Evident	3
Curriculum and Planning	1200	4.60	Very Evident	2
Assessment and Reporting	1200	4.61	Very Evident	1
Total		4.59	Very Evident	

While table 2 shows teachers also rated the same domains content knowledge and pedagogy 4.58, Learning Environment and Diversity of Learners 4.60, Curriculum and Planning 4.61, Assessment and Reporting 4.62 and having a total mean average of 4.60 which also means very Evident.

Table 3

SUMMARY OF RESPONSES OF SCHOOL HEADS AND TEACHERS ON THE DIFFERENT DOMAINS

Domain	School Head	WM	Teachers	WM	Total WM	Interpretation	Rank
Content Knowledge and Pedagogy	28	4.60	1200	4.56	4.58	Very Evident	4
Learning Environment and Diversity of Learners	28	4.61	1200	4.59	4.60	Very Evident	3
Curriculum and Planning	28	4.62	1200	4.60	4.61	Very Evident	2
Assessment and Reporting	28	4.62	1200	4.61	4.62	Very Evident	1
Total		4.61		4.59	4.60	Very Evident	

Furthermore table 3 presents the responses of school heads and teachers were combined the results shows that Assessment and Reporting was rank 1 (4.62 WM), Curriculum and Planning as rank 2 (4.61 WM), Learning Environment and Diversity of Learners as rank 3 (4.60 WM) and content knowledge and pedagogy as rank 4 (4.58) with a total Weight mean of 4.60 which also interpreted as Very Evident.

SOP 3. Based on the findings, what Professional Development Plan maybe proposed?

A Professional Development Plan was developed to served as guide and template of the school heads and teachers to sustain the best practices on RPMS-PPST.

SOP 4. What is the future plan of the XY for the Professional Development of teachers?

- Sustainability of the best practices of all school heads and teachers on RPMS PPST was highly encourage.
- Equipped teachers and school heads the new trends I teaching and learning.

XI. Conclusion

After the conduct of the study both teachers (WM 4.59) and school heads (WM 4.61) agreed that school heads provides technical assistance to teachers while the teachers received TA from their school heads with 4.60 total weighted mean and interpreted as very evident.

X. Recommendations

- Sustainability of the best practices of all school heads and teachers on RPMS PPST was highly encourage.
- Capacitate more master teachers to provide technical assistant to teachers in terms of strategies in teaching and learning to pupils.
- Parallel study may be conducted in providing technical assistance to teachers.

XII. Plans for Dissemination

The finding/s of this study will be echoed to the school heads of Trece Martires City for their review and serve as their spring board in giving technical assistance to their teachers, serve as their guide in crafting programs and projects in strengthening the teaching competencies for teachers and, for teachers to guide them to improve their teaching competencies for the benefit of their clientele.

XIII. References

Dr. Mark Anthony Cenas Pa-alisbo (2017) The 21st Century and Job Performance of Teachers. Journal of Education and Practice ISSN 2222-1735 (paper) ISSSN 2222-288x (online). Vol. 8, No. 32, 2017.

Jelena maksimivic and Nevena Dimic (2016) University of Nis, and Belgrade, Digital Technology and teachers' competence for its application in the classroom. Research in Pedagogy. Vol.6 No. 2, pp.59-71.

Results-Based Performance Management System Manual for Teachers and School Heads

Anna Marie S. Aranzanzo (2012) Instructional Competencies of Public Elementary Teachers: Input for Individual Plan for Professional Development IPPD, Eulogio "Amang" Rodreguez Institute of Science and Technology Nagtahan Sampaloc, Manila, Philippines.

BEI GRIN MACHT SICH IHR WISSEN BEZAHLT

- Wir veröffentlichen Ihre Hausarbeit, Bachelor- und Masterarbeit

- Ihr eigenes eBook und Buch - weltweit in allen wichtigen Shops

- Verdienen Sie an jedem Verkauf

Jetzt bei www.GRIN.com hochladen und kostenlos publizieren